Camino Eats for the Solo Vegan

James S. Peet

First Printing: 2019
Enumclaw WA 98022

ISBN: 978-0-9996093-8-5

Cover photos courtesy of Becky Rush-Peet
Cover design by Jeanine Henning

To *el Camino*

Contents

INTRODUCTION

About this book

This cookbook is a lot different than most, mainly because it's designed for the vegan Pilgrim (*Peregrino*) making a pilgrimage along one of the many routes of the *Camino de Santiago*. It's not just for vegans, though. Just about every recipe can be adapted to add seafood, poultry, or meat (for the carnivorous amongst us).

I've been camping since I was five (over half a century!) and backpacking since I was ten. I also spent a couple of months traveling around the United States on a motorcycle, camping out the entire time. I've walked the *Camino de Santiago*, so I'm pretty knowledgeable on the whole "cooking on the road/trail" thing.

Most of the recipes focus on suppers (or dinners, for those of you who call the final meal of the day that). Most breakfasts and lunches take place on the road, so there are very few breakfast recipes, and no lunch recipes (other than leftovers). Enjoy the walk and have a picnic of a vegetable *bocadilla* or one of the *menu del dia* at a bar or cafe. If you're vegan, you already know how to find vegan restaurants, but for those not familiar with this task, check out HappyCow (www.happycow.net) or do a Google Maps search near you for vegan restaurants. I find many an amazing vegan restaurant this way (even in Spain).

There are 11 main entrees that can be cooked in the pot/cup combination I recommend, so if you follow one of the guides that recommends doing the *Camino Frances* in 33 days, that means you'll only need to cook each meal three times. This, along with communal meals and dining out means you won't be eating the same thing over and over again. I've also included two microwaveable meals with multiple permutations, so even if a stove isn't available, and a microwave is, you won't suffer.

These recipes are all scalable, which means if you want to do a communal meal, just multiply the ingredients by the number of servings. For example, if a recipe calls for 1/2 can of beans, and you're serving four people, then use two cans of beans.

All directions utilize the recommended pot, cup, and utensils for measurements. Both the Toaks 450ml cup and the Snow Peak 700ml pot I recommend have internal markings for measurements. You will see most of the recipes using ounces (oz) instead of milliliters (ml) because the recipe just worked out better that way when I developed them. A spoonful refers to a level spoon of the size of a Sea-to-Summit Delta Cutlery spoon or a Light-my-Fire plastic spork. A heaping spoonful means stack the spoon until it can't hold any more.

For beginners, here are a few cooking terms to know. A *pinch* means the amount you can grasp between your index finger and your thumb. A *dash* means a shake of the shaker (e.g., shake the pepper shaker once or twice over the food). *Minced* means very finely chopped, *diced* means chopped, but not as small as minced. *Chopped* is basically cut up into chunks, the largest of the cuttings. *Incorporate* means to mix everything together until they are fully mixed.

Most vegetables can be bought at local stores (*tiendas*), supermarkets (*supermercados*) or greengrocers (*fruterias*). Some of the items (e.g., seitan, tofu, tempeh, or vegan meat substitutes) can only be bought in larger towns, so plan your meals according to what's available. One of the bigger stores throughout Spain that has a healthy selection of vegan foods (even prepared vegan dishes) is *El Corte Ingles*. Other national chains are *Mercadona* and *Consum*. Use Google Maps or other mapping software to find them - usually in the larger towns and cities. Health food stores (*Herbolario* or *Herbolaro*) also carry many of the items and can be found in many larger towns and cities.

There are also packaged vegan meals that one can find in the larger towns and cities, which are great for both the stove-top and the microwave. Be sure to check the ingredients, though. I provide a list some ingredients to watch out for in the *Oil and Other Stuff* section of this book.

I also include the Spanish names for every ingredient used in this book (*italicized*), so it should make your life a little better if you have limited Spanish speaking skills.

¡Buen Camino y buen provecho!

Equipment

This cookbook supposes you're walking the *Camino de Santiago*, where *albergues* and hostels abound, usually with some sort of kitchen available. Unfortunately, not all *albergues* or hostels have kitchen utensils (i.e., pots and pans), and there's no sense carrying the entire kitchen (with sink) with you, so these recipes have been developed with the minimalist kitchen that I think you'll need to carry in mind. This includes:

– **700ml or 750ml titanium pot with lid and measurements on the side**. I prefer the Snow Peak 700ml pot because of the unique design that allows one to drain the pot with the lid on. Another alternative is the Toaks 750ml pot). Snow Peak - 4.8 oz/136g - about $36 on Amazon; Toaks 3.6 oz/103g - about $35 on Amazon.
– **450ml titanium cup with lid** (Toaks - or something similar) - make sure it's a single-wall cup (*not* double-wall insulated as it would interfere with cooking) with measurements on the side - 3.2 oz/70g - about $25 on Amazon
– **Knife, fork, and spoon**. I use the Sea-to-Summit Delta cutlery set, which is made from food grade fiberglass reinforced nylon and can withstand the heat of boiling water - 1 oz/29g and about $11 on Amazon. But a single plastic spork will also work, available on Amazon for about $2. If you're worried about plastic melting in the pot while cooking,4 then I suggest a titanium or bamboo spoon or bamboo spork.
– **Ceramic knife** (4-5" blade with blade cover/sheath) - of course, you can carry a Swiss army knife, a steel knife, or a folding knife if you like - I just prefer the ceramic knife for cutting vegetables over a folding knife (it's a safety issue to me). Weight on these is usually less than 2 oz/57g and they can be bought on Amazon for about $5. You might want to put it inside a rigid container (e.g., a tube) to prevent the blade from snapping. I found a kitchen drain pipe, cut down to size, was ideal (about $4 at the local hardware store). I slip the sheathed knif4.8e inside it wrapped in foam insulation usually used to insulate water pipes in houses.

- **Plastic cutting mat or board** (Coughlin makes a very thin, light one, 8.5"x11"/21.6cm x 28 cm - 1.6 oz/45g and about $6 on Amazon - you could cut it in half if desired)
- **Can opener** - a small, backpacking one, or the one on a Swiss Army knife. I recommend the venerable P-38 can opener (aka, "the John Wayne"), at less than half-an-ounce, it's worth it. You can pick up a couple on Amazon for about $4-5.
- **Small locking, leak-proof plastic food container**. I have a 4-cup Snap Lock model by Progressive. It great for keeping leftovers, carrying fresh fruit and veggies, and has the added benefit of being microwave safe. That means, in those rare times there are no other cooking facilities other than a microwave (*microhondo*), at least you'll be able to cook something (even if it's only Ramen). It's only 3.1 oz/88g and runs about $9 on Amazon.
- **Small fluid container** (3 oz) for olive oil.
- **Quart sized Ziploc bag** to hold snack sized Ziploc bags for spices.

Altogether, your basic kitchen should run you between $85 and $100. Less if you hunt for bargains.

An optional piece of equipment is a small propane stove with small fuel canister (not necessary, but you never know - weighs about 8 ounces). I carry one (mainly because it allows me to make coffee in the morning at places where the kitchen is locked up when I get up in the morning). You can carry the canister and stove in the 700ml cup and put the 450ml cup in your mesh bottle pocket on the side of your backpack and nest a bottle in it or you can nest the stove in the 450ml cup and the 450ml cup in the 700ml cup.

Another optional piece of equipment is a Swiss Army Knife. I carry one all the time, so this is a no-brainer for me. Along with the can opener, it's got a bottle opener, two blades, and a corkscrew (handy for those bottles of *vino tinto*, which will help make you more friends along the *Camino*).

Including my Swiss Army Knife, stove, and fuel, my entire kitchen weighs 28.4 oz/805g. Without the stove and fuel, it's about 20 oz/567g. If you're into the ultra-lightweight load, then you can eliminate everything except the two cups, plastic spork, and some sort of cutting utensil to cut the weight down to 8 oz/28g or so. I recommend a Swiss Army Knife with at least one blade and a can opener, such as the Victorinox Bantam. Other good choices are the Victorinox Waiter, Recruit, and Spartan (my SAK of choice). Other people recommend an Opinel folding knife with corkscrew (plentiful along the *Camino*).

Complete Kitchen

Basic Kitchen

Ingredients

Spices

These are the spices used in the recipes. Some of these can be found in *albergue* kitchens occasionally.

Basil (*albahaca*)
Cumin (*comino*)
Ground cayenne (*polvo de pimento de cayena*)
Chili powder (*polvo de chile*)
Garlic powder (*polvo de ajo*)
Oregano (*orégano*)
Black Pepper (*pimienta negra*)
Crushed red pepper (*pimientos rojos molidos*)
Salt (*sal*)
Smoked paprika (*pimentón ahumado*)
Thyme (*tomillo*)
Turmeric (*cúrcuma*)

You might want to store each spice in a small, snack-sized Ziploc style bag separately and combine them in a quart-sized bag. They're lightweight, re-usable, and you can compress the air out and roll them up, thereby saving room in your pack. You should even be able to stuff them in the 450ml cup if you don't carry a portable stove.

Vegetables & Grains

These are the vegetables used in these recipes.

Avocado (*aguacate*)
Barley (*cebada*)
Beans (*frijoles*)
Carrot (*zanahoria*)
Celery (*apio*)
Cilantro (*cilantro*)

Corn (*maiz*)
Cucumber (*pepino*)
Garlic (*ajo*)
Green beans (*judias*)
Green pepper (*pimientos verdes*)
Lentils (*lentejas*)
Lettuce (*lechuga*)
Mushroom (*el champiñón*)
Oats (*los copos de avena* or *la avena enrollado*)
Onion (*cebolla*)
Peas (*guisantes*)
Peppers (*pimientos*)
Potato (*papa* or *patata*)
Red pepper (*pimiento rojo*)
Rice (*arroz*)
Instant rice (*arroz instantáneo*)
Spinach (*espinacas*)
Tomato (*tomate*)
Turnip tops (*grelos*)
Sweet potato (*boniato*)
Wild mushroom (*seta*)
Zucchini (*calabacin*)

Fresh Fruit

Fresh Fruit (*la fruta fresca*) available on the *Camino* (sometimes only in season).

Orange (*la naranja*)
Lemon (*el limón*)
Nut (*la nuez*)
Banana (*el plátano*)
Apple (*la manzana*)
Grape (*la uva*)
Berries (*las bayas*)
Apricot (*el ablaricoque*)
Pear (*la pera*)
Peach (*el durazno*)

Plum (*la ciruela*)
Quince (*el membrillo*)
Avocado (*el aguacate*)
Pomegranate (*la granada*)

Oil and Other Ingredients

These are some other things included in these recipes. You might wish to carry small containers of the oils and sauces, but buy the rest as you need them. As with spices, some can sometimes be found in *albergue* kitchens.

Olive oil (*aceite de oliva*)
Soy sauce (*salsa de soja*)
Lemon juice (*jugo de limón*)
Red wine (*vino tinto*) - this should be bought in the usual 750ml size - great for cooking, drinking, and sharing.
Balsamic vinaigrette (*Vinagre balsámico*)
Textured vegetable protein (*Proteína vegetal texturizada*)
Vegetable bouillon cube (*cubo de caldo de vegetal*)
Nutritional yeast (*levadura nutrcional*)

Tofu (*tofu*)
Seitan (*seitán*)
Tempeh (*tempeh*)
Nut butter (cashew, peanut, almond, etc.) (*mantequilla de nueces*)
Cashew butter (*crema de maní* or *mantequilla de maní*)
Peanut butter (*crema de anacardo* or *mantequilla de anacardo*)
Almond butter (*crema de almendras* or *mantequilla de almendras*)

Soy milk (*la leche de soja* or *bebida de soja*)
Almond milk (*la leche de almemdras* or *bebida de almendras*)
Rice milk (*bebida de arroz*)
Soy yogurt (*yogur de soja*)
Coconut milk (*leche de coco*)

Tomato paste (*pasta de tomate*)

Flour (*harina*)
Corn starch (*almindón de maiz*)
Sugar (*la azúgar*)
Brown sugar (*la azúgar morena*)
Nuts (*las nueces*)
Ground flaxseed (*semillas de linaza*)
Hemp seeds (*las semillas de cáñamo*)
Dried fruit(*la fruta seca*)
Pasta (*las pastas*)
Dried coconut flakes/chips (*coco seco*)

Non-Vegan Food Vocabulary

Some ingredients to watch out for if you're a strict vegan (look for these on the packaging of prepared products):

Dairy (*lactosa*)
Dairy products (*productos de lactos*)
Milk (*la leche*)
Cheese (*el queso*)
Yogurt (*el yogur*)
Eggs (*los huevos*)
Honey (*el miel*)

Look for the word *sin* when buying prepackaged meals - this means *without*. So, *sin huevos* means *without eggs*. *Hace con huevos* means *Made with eggs*. If you don't eat sugar, look for the phrase *sin azúgar*

BREAKFASTS

Oatmeal

Ingredients

8 oz Water
4 oz Oats

Directions

Cooking oatmeal is pretty straightforward. It's a two to one ratio (two parts of water to one part of oats). Get the water boiling, add oats, and reduce the temperature to the lowest setting. Simmer for 10 minutes, stirring occasionally.

Optional ingredients to add:

Sugar
Brown sugar
Milk (soy or almond)
Honey
Nuts

Fresh fruit
Berries
Ground flaxseed
Hemp seeds

Muesli

Ingredients

4 oz Uncooked oats
Nuts - a handful
Dried fruit - a handful
8 oz Milk - soy or almond

Directions

Add the ingredients the night before and refrigerate. Eat in the morning.

Optional ingredients to add:

Dried coconut flakes/chips
Yogurt

Cacao nibs
Sugar

SOUPS

Caldo de Gallego (Galician Soup)

This isn't quite the same as you'll find on the Camino, as there is no ham or chorizo, but it comes pretty danged close.

Ingredients

½ can white beans drained
1 vegetable bouillon cube
water

1 small or ½ medium potato - peeled and diced
1 medium carrot - peeled and sliced or diced
1 garlic clove - minced
Olive oil - 1 spoonful

Handful of turnip greens - chopped
¼ spoonful smoked paprika
Pinch of salt

Directions

Mix beans, vegetable cube, and water to the 700ml pot and bring to a boil over medium heat. The water should cover the beans, with enough left over to cover the remaining ingredients when added. Add the potato, carrot, garlic, and olive oil. Cover and simmer 15 minutes. Add the remaining ingredients, cover, and simmer for another 5 minutes.

Optional ingredients to add:

Vegan ham or chorizo   Chard
Celery   Kale

Bean Soup

Ingredients

½ can beans (preferably white beans)
1 vegetable bouillon cube
Water (see directions for amount)
1 medium carrot - sliced
1 celery stick - sliced
Pinch or dash of pepper
Pinch or dash of salt

Directions

Add the ingredients to the 700ml pot and bring to a boil over
medium heat. The water should cover all the ingredients, with
additional water to spare. Cover and simmer 20 minutes.

Optional ingredients to add:

Basil
Ground cayenne
Oregano
Smoked paprika
Thyme
Mushroom
Onion

Peas
Wild mushroom
Zucchini
Textured vegetable protein
Tofu
Seitan
Tempeh

Minestrone

Ingredients

½ can beans (cannellini, chickpea, or white beans) drained
4 oz. or a handful of pasta (penne or macaroni)
1 spoonful olive oil
1 garlic clove - minced
¼ onion - diced
1 vegetable bouillon cube
8 oz water
1 medium carrot - sliced
1 celery stick - sliced
1 medium tomato - diced
Handful of spinach or kale - chopped
Pinch of dried basil
Pinch of dried oregano
Pinch or dash of pepper
Pinch or dash of salt

Directions

Sauté the garlic, onion, celery, and carrots over medium high heat in the 700ml pot until tender. Add basil and oregano and stir. Add vegetable cube and water, cover, and bring the mixture to a boil. Add the beans and pasta and return to a boil. Reduce heat, cover, and simmer for 10-12 minutes (until pasta is cooked to your preference). Add the tomato and spinach, then flavor with salt and pepper.

Optional ingredients to add:

Basil
Ground cayenne
Smoked paprika
Mushroom
Onion

Wild mushroom
Textured vegetable protein
Seitan
Tempeh

Raman (everyone's stand-by meal)

Ingredients

Water - 1/3 of a 700ml pot.
Package of instant Ramen - break into pieces

Directions

Add the spice packet to the water. Bring the water to a boil, add the packet of broken Raman and cook on boiling for three minutes. If you're going to add other items, do so at the same time you add the Raman. If you're not, then why did you buy this book? Liven up your Raman with healthy stuff listed below!

Add the following ingredients if you want them (chop everything up into small, bite-sized bits).

Celery
Green pepper
Corn
Textured vegetable protein
Mushroom
Garlic
Peppers
Cilantro

Tofu
Scallions
Zucchini
Peas
Seitan
Tempeh
Soy sauce
Hot sauce

SAUCES

Marinara Sauce

Ingredients

2 heaping spoonfuls tomato paste
½ tomato - diced (and seeded if you don't like the seeds)
Pinch of basil
Pinch of oregano
Dash of salt
1 clove of Garlic
1 large Mushroom - sliced
1/8 small onion - diced
6 oz water (plus just a little more)
1 spoonful of Olive oil

Directions

Use the 450ml cup for this recipe. Sauté garlic, onion, and mushroom in garlic oil over medium heat. Add remaining ingredients (except basil), bring to a boil, cover and simmer for 10 minutes. Add basil just before serving.

Optional ingredients to add:

Olives - whole, sliced or chopped. I prefer black olives due to their milder flavor. It's your dinner - you choose what color olive you want.

Alfredo Sauce

Ingredients

2 spoonfuls of flour
1 spoonful of olive oil
Pinch of garlic
4-6 oz of soy or almond milk
Dash of salt
½ spoonful of nutritional yeast
Dash of lemon juice
Dash of soy sauce

Directions

Heat oil on low heat, then add the flour and mix until flour is fully incorporated. Add the garlic. Continue stirring and slowly add the soy/almond milk until all the milk has been added. Once all the milk has been added, add the remaining ingredients, stirring constantly, until everything is incorporated and it begins to bubble. At this point, it's done. It should be a little thick, just like real Alfredo sauce.

Basic Salsa/Pico de Gallo

Ingredients

1 tomato - diced
¼ onion - diced
1 oz cilantro - chopped
1 clove garlic - minced
1/3 spoonful lime juice
1/3 jalapeno pepper - minced (or select amount to taste)
Pinch of salt

Directions

Mix everything together and enjoy.

Cheese Sauce

Ingredients

4 oz vegan milk (soy/almond/coconut)
3-4 heaping spoonfuls of nutritional yeast
1/4 spoonful of garlic powder
1/2 spoonful of salt

Directions

Mix all the ingredients in the cup. Heat over low heat until bubbling. For microwaving, mix everything in a microwaveable container and microwave on high for 1 minute.

ENTREES

Lentil stew

Ingredients

4 oz dried lentils
8 oz water
1 medium carrot - diced
¼ medium onion or ½ small onion - diced
1-2 mushrooms - sliced
Pinch or dash of Salt
Pinch or dash of Pepper
1 clove of garlic
2 spoonfuls of Olive oil

Tip

To measure the water/lentils, use the 450ml cup and add lentils up the 4 oz line. Transfer the lentils to the 700ml pot, and add water to the 450ml cup until it is at the 8 oz line. Return the lentils to the 450ml cup, then use the 700ml pot to sauté the veggies. Add the water/lentils to the 700ml cup when the veggies are sautéed.

Directions

Sauté onion, garlic, and mushroom in olive oil. Add carrot, lentils, and water and bring to a boil. Add salt and pepper, cover and simmer 20 minutes (longer for softer lentils).

Optional ingredients to add:

This is a basic recipe that can easily be modified by adding a variety of vegetables and spices (see the next page).

Celery

Tomato

Potato

Smoked paprika

Green pepper

Soy sauce

Curry powder

Beans and rice

Ingredients

½ can beans (black, kidney, or pinto) - drained
4 oz. rice
Water - see required amount in directions
½ spoonful cumin
Dash of ground cayenne
Pinch of oregano
Pinch or dash of salt

Directions

Fill 700ml pot to the 4 oz mark with rice. Add water until it reaches the 12 oz mark. Add the beans and spices (and any other ingredients you like). Bring the mixture to a boil then cover and reduce heat to low. Simmer for 15-20 minutes (according the cooking directions for your specific rice)

Optional ingredients to add:

Avocados - sliced
Diced peppers
Celery
Mushrooms
Cilantro

File powder
Thyme
Salsa
Seitan

Recommended Side Dish

Salad with some cruciform vegetables (spinach, kale, etc.)

Chili with Rice

Ingredients

1 spoonful Olive oil
1 clove Garlic
¼ onion - diced
½ can beans - drained
½ spoonful Cumin
1 spoonful Chili powder (I prefer a heaping spoonful)
1 medium tomato - diced
1 vegetable bouillon cube
½ 450ml cup water

4 oz rice
8 oz water

Directions

Cook using the 700ml pot with lid.

Sauté onion and garlic in olive oil over medium low heat until onions are translucent. Add rest of the ingredients and put the lid on. Bring to a boil. Once boiling, reduce heat to simmer and cook for 20 minutes. The chili will be quite soupy when done, so if you like, you can drain the excess moisture or eat it as a chili soup. You can also add a thickener, such as flour or corn starch (less than a spoonful).

Cook the rice in your 450ml cup. Instant rice works well for this (and is faster). For normal rice, bring the water to a boil, add the rice, cover and simmer for 20 minutes.

Optional ingredients to add:

Rice   Smoked paprika
Celery   Green pepper

Crushed red pepper	Tofu
Corn	Tomato paste
Seitan	TVP
Tempeh	Mushroom
	Flour

1/2 spoonful Corn starch - mix with a couple of spoonfuls of water then add to the chili and mix in - serves as a thickener

Barley Stew

Ingredients

4 oz barley
1 clove garlic - minced
½ small or ¼ medium onion - diced
½ carrot - diced
½ stick celery
2 mushrooms
1 vegetable bouillon cube
1 spoonful olive oil
1 450ml cup of water
Pinch or dash of Salt
Pinch or dash of Pepper

Directions

Sauté onion, mushroom, and garlic in olive oil until onions are transparent (3-5 minutes). Add the remaining ingredients, bring to a boil, then cover and simmer for 45-50 minutes.

Because of the longer cooking time, this is a dish best prepared when there are few vying for the kitchen.

Optional ingredients to add:

Cilantro
Green beans
Green pepper
Peas
Peppers

Potato
Red pepper
Spinach
Zucchini

Vegetable Stew

Ingredients

1 medium potato (on the smallish side) - peeled and cut into small chunks
1 medium carrot - sliced
¼ medium onion - diced
½ stick celery - sliced
1 large or 2 small mushrooms - sliced
1 vegetable bouillon cube
450 ml of water (enough to fill the 700ml pot almost to the top)
Pinch or dash of Salt
Pinch or dash of Pepper

Directions

Place all the ingredients in a pot, add the water, bring to a boil, then cover and simmer for 20 minutes.

Tip

I recommend mixing all the vegetables before putting them in the pot, and put the bouillon cube in the middle of the mixture.

Optional ingredients to add:

Cashews
Ground flaxseed
Garlic
Green beans
Hemp seeds
Peas
Peppers
Seitan

Spinach
Sweet potato (substitute for potato)
Tempeh
Tofu
Tomato
Wild mushroom
Zucchini

Jambalaya

Ingredients

1 spoonful Olive oil
¼ onion - diced
¼ green pepper
½ celery stick
1 clove garlic - minced
½ can beans (red are best) - drained
1 spoonful tomato paste
¼ spoonful Cumin
1 spoonful Chili powder
1 medium tomato - diced and seeded
1 vegetable bouillon cube
Pinch of dried Thyme
Seitan (or other vegan meat substitute)
4 oz. rice
8 oz water

Directions

Sauté onion, garlic, celery, and green pepper in olive oil over medium heat until they begin to soften. Add another spoonful of olive oil if necessary, to prevent burning. Stir in the tomato paste. Add the remaining ingredients except the seitan. Bring to a boil, cover, and reduce heat to low. Simmer until rice is almost done (about 20 minutes, depending on the rice), then add the seitan (recover the pot).

Optional ingredients to add:

Mushrooms   File powder
Cilantro

Mushroom Stroganoff

Ingredients

1 spoonful of olive oil
¼ onion, diced
2 large mushrooms - sliced, diced, or cut big
1 cup pasta
8 oz water
1 vegetable bouillon cube
½ spoonful of nutritional yeast
Dash of black pepper
Dash of salt
Dash of lemon juice (best squeezed from a fresh lemon)
1 heaping spoonful of nut butter (cashew, peanut, almond, whatever)

Directions

Sauté onions in olive oil in pot 3-5 minutes. Add pasta, mushrooms, water, vegetable bouillon cube, nutritional yeast, salt, and pepper. Be sure everything is covered with water (you may need to add more). Bring to a boil, then cover and simmer for 15 minutes (stir to prevent sticking). Turn off heat, add lemon juice and nut butter (salt if desired). Stir until completely incorporated.

Optional ingredients to add:

Textured vegetable protein   Tempeh
Seitan

Recommended Side Dish

Salad with some cruciform vegetables (spinach, kale, etc.)

Red Wine Pasta

Ingredients

Handful of pasta (any pasta can be used)
3/4 filled 700ml cup of water

Spoonful of olive oil
2 mushrooms - sliced
½ stick celery
1 clove garlic - minced
Seitan or tempeh - cut into small cubes (you'll have to guesstimate how much you want)
Dash of oregano
Dash of basil
Red wine

Directions

Cook pasta in water according to directions. While pasta is cooking, combine remaining ingredients (except red wine) in 450ml cup and cook until celery and mushrooms are tender. Add red wine until vegetables are barely covered and simmer until pasta is done. Be sure to taste the wine during the cooking process (but leave some for cooking!). Drain the pasta, coat it with olive oil (i.e., drizzle a lit bit on the top and mix it in), and add the vegetable/wine mixture to the pasta.

Optional ingredients to add:

Textured vegetable protein   Cashews
Tofu

Recommended Side Dish

Salad with some cruciform vegetables (spinach, kale, etc.)

Penne Pasta

Ingredients

Water - ¾ full for the 700ml pot
Penne pasta ½ full for the 450ml cup - set aside (you'll need the cup for cooking)
Olive oil
½ small zucchini - diced
2 Mushrooms - sliced
4-5 Olives - sliced

Directions

Fry the garlic, chopped mushrooms, zucchini, and olives in the 700ml pot, stirring constantly (but don't melt your spoon). Add salt and pepper to taste. Once it's done, remove it from the stove and empty the contents of the pot into the 450ml cup. Cover the cup with the lid. If you want to, wrap something around it (like a shirt or towel) to keep it warmer.

For the pasta, boil water in 700ml pot. Add less than a spoonful of olive oil and the penne pasta. Cook the pasta 8-14 minutes (this is based on your desire for al dente (slightly undercooked) or a softer textured pasta. Drain (using the Snow Peak pot lid) and coat with olive oil.

Add the vegetables to the pasta in the large pot. If you plan on having sauce with it, cover the pot and cook the sauce in the 450ml cup to cook it. It should stay warm until the sauce is ready.

Optional Ingredients

Marinara sauce   Alfredo sauce

Arroz con lo que sera

I call this recipe *Arroz con lo que sera* because it's basically whatever you want the *lo que sera* to be, whether it be seitan, tofu, tempeh, cashews, or meat/fish (your choice).

Ingredients

1 spoonful olive oil
1/8 medium onion - diced
¼ bell pepper, seeded and diced
1 garlic clove - minced
4 oz rice
8 oz water
1 vegetable bouillon cube
1 small tomato - diced and seeded
Handful of fresh peas
2-3 pimiento stuffed olives - sliced
Two spoonfuls of salsa
Pinch of dried oregano
Pinch of ground cumin
Pinch of turmeric

Directions

Sauté the onion and bell pepper over medium heat until the onion is translucent (3-5 minutes) stirring constantly. Add garlic, oregano, cumin, and turmeric and sauté another minute or two. If you decide to include a protein source (tempeh, seitan, cashews, or meat), add it with the garlic, oregano, etc.

Add the rice, water, vegetable cube, and tomato. Bring the mixture to a boil, then cover and simmer 20 minutes (or until rice is tender). Stir occasionally. Add the remaining ingredients, mix everything up, cover and cook another five minutes (see the next page).

Optional ingredients to add:

Seitan

Tempeh

Cashews

Green beans

Chickpea Stew

Since chickpeas (also known as garbanzo beans) are ubiquitous in Spain, this is an easy dish to get the ingredients for.

Ingredients

1 spoonful of Olive oil
¼ medium onion or 1/2 small onion - diced
1-2 mushrooms - sliced
1 clove of garlic - minced
½ potato - peeled and diced
1 heaping spoonful of tomato paste
Pinch or dash of cayenne pepper
½ spoonful of cumin
Pinch of oregano
½ can chickpeas
8 oz water
1 vegetable bouillon cube
1 tomato - diced and seeded
Pinch or dash of salt
Pinch or dash of ground black pepper

Directions

Sauté onion, garlic, and mushroom in olive oil over medium heat until the onions are translucent (about 3-5 minutes). Add potatoes, tomato paste, cayenne pepper, cumin, and oregano. Stir for about 30 seconds. Add in the remaining ingredients and mix. Bring to a boil, cover, and reduce heat to a simmer. Simmer for 20 minutes, then add salt and pepper (to taste).

If you would like a thicker stew, mix a spoonful of flour with three spoonfuls of water, and stir the mixture into the stew before serving.

MICROWAVE MEALS

Beans and Rice

I don't normally recommend instant rice, but microwaving regular rice is a hit or miss proposition (which I mostly miss), so this recipe calls for instant rice.

Ingredients

150g of instant rice
150g of water
½ can beans (kidney or pinto) - drained
½ spoonful cumin
Dash of ground cayenne
Dash of oregano
Dash of salt

Directions

Add the rice and water to the microwaveable container. Microwave uncovered on high for 3 minutes. If you only have one microwavable container, remove the rice and put it into the 450ml cup and cover it. Put the beans and remaining ingredients into a microwaveable container. Mix up the ingredients, then put the cover over the container (but don't seal it) and microwave on high for 2 minutes. Stir up the ingredients again, add the rice, and mix everything together.

Optional ingredients to add:

Diced peppers
Celery
Mushrooms
Cilantro

File powder
Seitan
Salsa
Avocados – sliced

Recommended Side Dish

Salad with some cruciform vegetables (spinach, kale, etc.)

Basic Bean Stuffed Potato (with options)

Ingredients

1 large potato
Salt to taste
Pepper to taste
½ spoonful Olive oil
1 spoonful nutritional yeast
½ can beans

Directions

Clean the potato by washing and scrubbing the outside. Poke it with a fork in several places (that way it won't explode in the microwave when the moisture inside expands rapidly due to heat - just in case you were wondering why). Wrap it in a damp paper towel, place it in the microwave (microhondo) and microwave on high until soft. This can be anywhere from 3 to 10 minutes (so you'll need to constantly check your potato).

Once cooked, remove the potato from the microwave. Microwave the beans for 1 to 2 minutes. Remove the towel from the potato and slice it open. Dice the inside of the potato, add the remaining ingredients, and stir it up a bit (mix things as best as you can).

Food for thought

This menu can be modified for a breakfast by using a sweet potato and adding fresh or dried fruit, cacao/chocolate nibs, date syrup, or whatever you fancy or is on hand.

Optional ingredients to add:

These are all the things you can easily add to make your potato yummy. If there's something you don't see, find it and add it.

After all, it's your potato, your tastes. Vegetables can be added raw or cut and cooked in the microwave to your desire (some like it al dente, and other like soft vegetables)

Basil
Beans - mashed (chickpeas are plentiful)
Carrot - diced
"Cheese" sauce
Ground cayenne
Celery - sliced
Cheese sauce (p. 20)
Chili powder
Cilantro - chopped

Onion - diced
Oregano
Peppers - diced
Crushed red pepper
Salsa
Seitan - diced (microwave on high 2-7 minutes in covered container)
Smoked paprika
Spinach- chopped

Corn
Cumin
Garlic - minced or whole
Green pepper - diced
Mushroom - sliced
Nuts (almond, pine, whatever is available)
Nut butter (peanut, almond, whatever is available)

Tempeh - diced (microwave on high 2-7 minutes in covered container)
Thyme
Tofu - diced (microwave on high 2-7 minutes in covered container)
Tomato - diced
Wild mushroom - sliced
Zucchini - diced

Recommended Side Dish

Salad with some cruciform vegetables (spinach, kale, etc.)

That's all Folks

Dear Reader,

Thanks for buying *Camino Eats for the Solo Vegan*. I hope you enjoyed it. As an independent author, I don't have a marketing department or the exposure of being on bookshelves, so if you enjoyed it, please help spread the word and support my writing by writing an Amazon review or telling a few friends about the book.

Thanks again,

James S. Peet
Enumclaw, Washington, USA

About the Author

James S. Peet is a modern-day Renaissance Man. He's lived on four continents, six countries, and visited countless more. He's been a National Park Service Ranger, a police officer, a tow-truck driver, a college instructor, a private investigator, a fraud examiner/forensic accountant, an inventor, and an entrepreneur. His other writing endeavors include the *Corps of Discovery* series (*Surveyor* and *Trekker*) set in the multiverse, several articles on modern sea piracy, economics, and the private investigation of fraud. He lives on the top of a small mountain in the foothills of Washington's Cascade Mountains with his wife, dogs, barn cats, and whatever adult daughter returns to the nest. He's attended 10 colleges and universities, two law enforcement academies, and has three degrees (all in geography) and multiple certificates (he really likes learning). He walked the Camino with his wife, both earning their *Compostelas* in 2018.

http://jamespeet.com

Printed in Great Britain
by Amazon